OPTIMIZE FOR GROWTH

OPTIMIZE FOR GROWTH

How to Scale Up Your Business, Your Network and You

Jonathan B. Smith

ISBN: 0692485317
ISBN 13: 9780692485316
Library of Congress Control Number: 2015910832
Chief Optimizer, New York, NY

Praise For *Optimize For Growth*

"Jonathan really captures the essence of 'working together' to define a compelling vision, comprehensive strategy, and relentless implementation plan to deliver profitable growth for all the company's stakeholders!"
Alan Mulally, Former President/CEO, Ford Motor Company

"Jonathan B. Smith truly understands the hurdles CEOs face as they try to grow their businesses. In this quick and powerful read, he describes three key elements they can use to optimize their success. It's a must read for every business owner who wonders how to get out of their own way and get the right resources to grow."
Gino Wickman, Author of the award-winning book *Traction* and Creator of EOS Worldwide

"In this quick read, Jonathan B. Smith describes three key ways to optimize growth. It's a must read for every business owner who wants to grow! Two likeable thumbs up!"
Dave Kerpen, *NY Times* Bestselling Author, *The Art of People*

"Any entrepreneur fortunate enough to work with Jonathan, learns his methods and techniques to achieve success and will discover a predictable plan for growth. With this book, there are no limits to the number of business owners who can benefit from his brilliance, determination, and model for success."

Cyndi Gave, President/CEO, The Metiss Group, Inc.

"If you are an Entrepreneur, Owner or CEO who has matured enough to finally realize you only have a finite number of days in your life, and, you really want to capture these to their fullest, then read this simple book and follow the path Jonathan lays out for us. It is a "can't miss" formula that my clients have been following for years. Jonathan just captures the pattern others know intuitively and spells it out for us. Thanks for putting this together, Mr. Smith!"

Walt Brown, Multi-company Entrepreneur, seasoned Coach and Peer Board Facilitator, focused as a Master EOS Implementer.

"Jonathan B. Smith is called the chief optimizer for a good reason. He dives in and shows you how to think differently, how to optimize resources to the fullest potential, including things that often go unnoticed and under valued. This book is a key tool for any entrepreneur looking for growth or solutions to everyday challenges that come with leading a company."

Amilya M. Antonetti, CEO AmA Productions

For my wife Doris
Who understands how to be a true partner

TABLE OF CONTENTS

CHAPTER 1

HITTING THE CEILING

Scale-up is so much harder than start-up.
DANIEL ISENBERG
PROFESSOR OF ENTREPRENEURSHIP
PRACTICE, BABSON GLOBAL

Dave Marinac's business hit the ceiling. He had built his company, ABC Packaging Direct (the maker of Stand Up Pouches), into a $2 million business and he did not know how to get it to $5 million. He was working 18 hours a day and the grit and the hard work that he had relied on to launch his business was not enough to continue growing it to the next level.

"I'm good at selling and plowing through work and making things happen," Dave shared. "But I'm not the best at managing people and staying on top of them to make sure work gets done. No one knows what their roles are and financially, it's a juggling match."

Dave wanted more than to grow his business from $2M to $5M. He wanted to take it to $25M. And, he knew that he did not have the tools, the structure, and the accountability to take it to the next level.

Like Dave, many growth-oriented entrepreneurs inevitably hit the ceiling. The creativity, tenacity, and downright heroism they use to build their companies take them out of the starting gate and around the first bend of the track. As profits grow, these entrepreneurs add employees, sign more customers, and develop new products. But at some point, their growth stalls. And when it does, they may have lost their momentum without adequate systems, processes, and organizational structure to optimize their growth.

ENTREPRENEURIAL ROADBLOCKS

You probably already know this: it is much easier to start up than to scale up. In my work with hundreds of entrepreneurial organizations, I've seen four primary barriers to growth:

People—Leaders are frustrated with employees, customers, vendors and/or partners. Nobody seems to listen, understand, or follow through. Teams wallow in dysfunction without clear roles, accountability, and interactions.
Profit—The business is not generating adequate profit to justify the time and effort that everything seems to take. Leaders do not have enough working capital to run the

day-to-day operations. Many fill this shortfall by taking on debt to fill the gap.

Control—Leaders feel as though they have lost control over their time, the market, or even their company. Instead of controlling the business, the business controls them.

Traction—Leaders spend more time putting out fires than sustaining growth with disciplined, repeatable, effective processes.

I experienced these barriers before I took a $500,000 business to $15 million and landed on that coveted Inc. 500 list. Often, the entrepreneur/CEO/visionary does everything in his or her power to fix the problems that stand in the way of growth. But while a degree of business heroism often builds the startup, it takes a different set of ingredients to scale up.

Unfortunately, many emerging growth businesses (those in the $2 to $50 million range) get mired in this stagnant phase because they are not sure how to solve their issues. They are reluctant to take a measured approach and further constrain their cash flow by making rash, short-term decisions in an effort to stem the pain. These businesses question the merit of what at face value appears to be yet another quick fix.

LOOKING OUTSIDE YOUR BUSINESS

Some high-growth teams, including my own and the ones we will discuss in this book, have chosen to leverage the wisdom of a set of trusted outsiders—people who have been *there* already, and who can accelerate personal and organizational learning curves. Such high-growth teams utilize these outside resources to support and build their own internal capabilities to achieve breakthrough growth.

As an analogy, I like to recall when I was a child and worked to repair a basement with my grandmother. We had to put temporary supporting columns up until the permanent columns were ready to be installed. Similarly, in an organization, if you don't have adequate resources on your own team, then these outside and trusted advisors can provide temporary support until you build the resources yourself. Organizations use these resources as a means of taking the elevator instead of the stairs to optimize their growth.

When Dave Marinac hit the ceiling with ABC Packaging Direct, one of his first realizations was that he needed to build a leadership team. He wasn't sure how to do this, so he enlisted an executive coach and talked to me about implementing an operating system for his business. It took time, effort, and patience, but Dave and the team that he created learned that with a good structure and the savvy use of outside experts, they could manage problems as they arose and create disciplined work habits.

"Now," Dave said, "When issues arise. It's not all or nothing. It's not the end of the world."

Over the course of the next 18 months, Dave's business grew 70%. He began to scale up.

THE OPTIMIZE FOR GROWTH MODEL DRIVES SCALE

We call the use of trusted outsiders the *Optimize for Growth Model*. It is the surest recipe to gain traction within your organization. That's often what it comes down to, isn't it? *You need traction.*

- My sales are great but I never seem to have enough cash on hand. (**Profit**)
- I used to know all of our customers and now I don't know them and feel I have no control over the business. (**Control**)
- I used to be able to meet with each prospect and close the deal. Now my Sales Manager says I'm stepping on her toes. (**People**)
- My people don't seem to understand me and follow through. (**People**)
- We have so many options we can't prioritize and focus our efforts. (**Traction**)

Entrepreneurs express many of these frustrations when I first meet with them. Like Dave Marinac, they have survived the hero's journey by their own sheer will and belief in their vision for the business. But does the rest of your organization share your vision? Do they know what it is? And, is your organization rallied around this shared vision with a disciplined process and approach to achieving and maintaining it?

When it comes down to it, entrepreneurs and their leadership teams must develop and continuously evolve three core areas in order to scale up:

1. An **operating system** so the business can run at scale instead of on the heroic efforts of the founder and leadership team.
2. A **peer network** to leverage the wisdom of business peers—similar to a board of advisors.
3. A **coach** to shore up leadership skills and blind spots.

Each of these three areas individually supports the entrepreneur's quest for personal and professional growth. Together, these amplify results and improve the overall chance for success.

THE OPTIMIZE FOR GROWTH MODEL

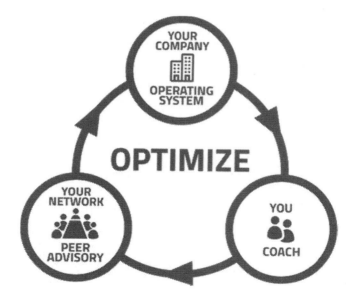

SUMMARY AND ORGANIZATION OF THE BOOK

Entrepreneurs often run fast to achieve high growth early on and then they hit the ceiling. Their chief issues stem from people issues, decreased profits, and lack of control and traction. In the rest of this book, we'll drill down into the three areas businesses must optimize for growth.

Chapter 2: Optimize Your Business—Implement a system of processes and controls, an "operating system," to give traction to your vision and develop a healthy team. This is the longest chapter since your business has so many components including vision, people, data, issues, process, and traction.[1]

Chapter 3: Optimize Your Network—Develop connections with experts and peers to leverage their perspectives. What peer advisory group should you join to give your organization the benefit of its own board of outside advisors?

Chapter 4: Optimize You—Find and utilize a coach or mentor to boost your personal leadership skills and give you individual traction. What types of coaches should you consider and how do you select the right one?

---

1 Gino Wickman, *Traction*, Benbella, 2011.

Chapter 5: Optimize Your Growth Today—Consider which area(s) of the Optimize for Growth system you will implement first to take the first step in achieving sustainable growth.

Whether you work with an implementer for an operating system, a peer group, or a coach first, you'll start to develop the discipline, structure, and team health to break through the ceiling. Each area of the Optimize for Growth Model is a powerful step that takes your business outside its internal stagnation to experts who have already "been there and done that" to achieve their own success.

In the end, the system has two chief goals: First, to give your business access to the trusted advisors who can help it optimize for growth. Second, to give your business the necessary tools to tackle the daily issues and barriers to growth. Each element of the Optimizer system drives a particular type of growth: profit, leadership, and personal momentum. These elements must all be developed on your journey to business success. Let's get started.

CHAPTER 2

OPTIMIZE YOUR BUSINESS

*Good business leaders create a vision, articulate
the vision, passionately own the vision, and
relentlessly drive it to completion.*
JACK WELCH
FORMER CHAIRMAN AND CEO OF GENERAL ELECTRIC

Vision drives your business. Ford Motor Company knows
something about corporate vision. When Alan Mulally
joined Ford as CEO from The Boeing Company in September
2006, the company was about to post a $5.6 billion quarterly
loss. To reverse Ford's downward spiral, Mulally created a plan
to simplify the product line and borrow money to ride out the
global economic crisis. He also created the One Ford Vision,
which specified how people would work together towards "one
team, one plan, one goal." Mulally's consistent articulation of
that vision to everyone, everywhere, gave legs to Ford's growth.

Joe Nocera commented on Mulally's vision in the *New York
Times* on June 2014 after interviewing Bryce Hoffman, author

of *American Icon: Alan Mulally and the Fight to Save Ford Motor Company.* "Once he had his vision for the company, he repeated it at the start of every meeting, whether the audience was Ford executives, securities analysts or journalists," he wrote.

Mulally told Paul W. Smith on WJR morning radio that he and Bill Ford agreed on

> *Pulling everybody together around a compelling vision and a strategy for Ford going forward, and then a plan to achieve it. Two, bringing a management system where everybody was included, everybody knew what the plan was, everybody knew what areas need special attention, and the culture change that would go with that...*

Ford's transition from losing $12.6 billion in 2006 to making $8.6 billion in 2013 can be directly attributed to this vision and its execution throughout a global organization. Imagine creating a compelling vision for your company, sharing it with everyone in the company, and tracking to it on a regular basis. Would that take your business from $5 million to $50 million? From $50 million to $200 million?

LACK OF SHARED VISION LEADS TO FAILURE

My own experience reflects the need for shared vision. In 2001, my first startup failed. At the time, I was a member of the Entrepreneur's Organization (EO), a global peer-to-peer network of entrepreneurs. I met Gino Wickman in my local

Detroit chapter. Gino was developing what would become the Entrepreneurial Operating System and we engaged him to help us smoke out why our business, 3D New Media, had stalled; why we couldn't seem to gain enough traction to grow. Like many emerging growth companies, we had hit the ceiling. As it turned out, we were doomed to fail.

Why? Because my three partners and I didn't share the same vision and core values. When Gino sat down with us, we discovered conflicts between what each of us wanted for the business—and for our lives. This lack of alignment caused a constant friction among the team. And, without a common vision, there is little to no chance of growth and continued success.

Core values, as Gino described them, provide the foundation from which a leadership team, and thus an organization, build a shared vision and execute against it for success. When a leadership team's core values are not aligned, things start to fall apart. As we would soon realize, when an organization probes into its core values, the leaders either come together, or break apart. We broke apart.

Fortunately, most companies I work with today do share core values: they just haven't gathered around a table to articulate and document them. They haven't utilized a trusted outsider or strategy execution coach to help them implement a disciplined cadence and related infrastructure, or operating system, on which to build their company. Without this operating system, most entrepreneurs and emerging growth companies hit the ceiling. They simply lack the tools for growth beyond a certain size.

OPTIMIZE YOUR BUSINESS WITH
AN OPERATING SYSTEM

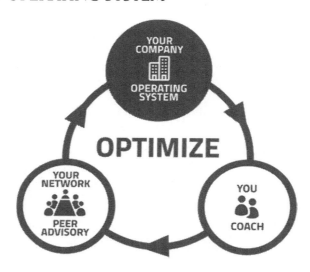

IMPLEMENT THE ENTREPRENEURIAL
OPERATING SYSTEM

By 2005, I was building my third startup, Wave Dispersion Technologies, Inc., a maritime fence designed to stop a Water Borne Improvised Explosive Device (WBIED). Initially, my father founded the business to stop beach erosion, but in managing the strategy and execution, I helped him turn it into an innovative defense system for clients ranging from the U.S. government to foreign sovereigns. Our vision and values were aligned.

By this time, Gino Wickman had founded the Entrepreneurial Operating System (EOS), which he describes in his book, *Traction, Get a Grip on Your Business* (Benbella 2011). Today, EOS Worldwide is a robust organization with a concrete methodology and set of tools that help thousands of emerging growth businesses develop the strategy and infrastructure they need to scale up. EOS played a critical role in my company's ability to grow from $500,000 to $15 million.

The EOS model addresses six key components every business needs to optimize for growth. In 2013, I became a full-time professional EOS Implementer to leverage my entrepreneurial experience to help companies clarify, simplify, and achieve their vision. In the remainder of this chapter, I will walk you through each of the six components and explain how and why to strengthen them for your business.

THE ENTREPRENEURIAL OPERATING SYSTEM (EOS)

The Chief Operating Officer (COO) at a life sciences firm I worked with said that he and his partners had tried several consultants over the years, but they continued to struggle with vision alignment, accountability, and personnel issues. Like many small to medium businesses, this leadership team had worked so hard to grow fast, benefitting from early success, that they hadn't yet developed the systems and processes to take their organization from a startup to a highly functioning organization capable of continuous breakthrough growth.

"The company's eleven years old," the COO said. "We've been through countless folks who haven't done anything with us." Bringing in EOS, "engaged every member of the executive team." Previously, each member of the executive team had quarterly goals. "At the beginning of the quarter, we would all agree they were doable and invariably, maybe 50% of them would get done," he shared. "After closing our first full quarter using EOS, 70% of the goals got accomplished."

NAIL YOUR VISION

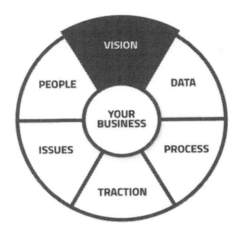

You'll notice that the EOS model begins with vision. As my colleagues and I learned in our experience at 3D New Media, a cohesive corporate vision based on shared core values can make or break your chance for growth. Shoring up your vision isn't just an exercise for entrepreneurs. Even major corporations like Ford—which clawed its way back from the brink of bankruptcy—have pinned their growth strategy on one vision to drive the organization forward.

START WITH YOUR CORE VALUES

Core values are the three to seven essential, guiding characteristics that define your organization's culture. They fuel the vision. They might include values such as integrity, innovative spirit, or a roll-up-your sleeves attitude. Once defined, it's important to repeat your core values often and use these as real standards; rules everyone must play by.

NETFLIX CORE VALUES MAP TO VALUE PROPOSITION

In 2009, Netflix co-founder and CEO Reed Hastings posted a presentation on SlideShare titled, Netflix Culture: Freedom and Responsibility. The 126 slides spell out a company culture and core values that directly tie to the Netflix core value proposition. After all, what distinguished Netflix against Blockbuster was the concept of having no due dates and no late fees for movie rentals. If you take the time to scroll through the presentation, you'll get to the part about why Netflix has no vacation policy ("we don't track hours worked, why track vacation?") and how process shouldn't be implemented at the expense of creativity and innovation.

Netflix seeks out talent that represents its core values so that it can give employees the freedom to innovate while expecting them to take the responsibility for hard work. It's kind of like having the ability to keep movies for an unlimited period as long as you return them or to watch as many movies at you want for a set fee.

When I conduct a two-day vision-building session with clients, we start by outlining their core values. In order to build a culture of people who will charge forward with your vision, it's important to be consistent and constantly articulate your values. Hire people with these values, and they are the ones you will keep. In his <u>video on Business Perpetuating Core Values</u>, Gino Wickman describes why it's so essential to hire people who share your core values, review them against the values, and share stories about how individual and company success stems from one of the values.

After the vision-building session, I give clients some homework: to create a core values speech. This is a one-page outline that clearly defines for everyone in the organization exactly what each of the company's core values means. The speech uses stories, analogies, and examples to help every leader talk about his or her core values in a clear and consistent way.

PUT THE RIGHT PEOPLE IN THE RIGHT SEAT

In 2009, Joseph Kopser was a Lieutenant Colonel in the U.S. Army living in Arlington, Virginia with a daily five-mile commute to the Pentagon. Each day, he wanted to determine the best way to get there. If it was sunny out, he might want to walk. Raining? He needed a cab. Or, was the Metro running on time? Essentially, he wanted a tool to show him the most efficient transportation option to get to work depending on his circumstances and time of day.

So, he founded RideScout along with his West Point classmate and former Army intelligence officer, Craig Cummings. The RideScout mobile app shows real-time information about transportation options including bus, bike, taxi, car share, rideshare, parking, and walking directions that are available at the moment you need them. The mobile app helps you get from point A to point B faster and smarter.

The two army veterans soon added two more former officers and friends and the four members of the leadership team then embarked on the hero's journey to launch RideScout in strategic cities as soon as possible. As often happens with startups among friends, family, and former colleagues, everyone pitched in, roles and responsibilities merged as these smart, driven leaders with the best of intentions worked hard to grow the company. Essentially, each of these men was accustomed to leading a battalion of 800 soldiers. Yet, translating those leadership skills into running their startup proved challenging. The 'I've got your back' foundation of the armed services can create barriers to growth in business.

"Initially there was more redundancy in what we were doing," co-founder Craig Cummings shared. "We had two team members operating both operations and business development. It was working but created some confusion."

RIDESCOUT BUILDS ACCOUNTABILITY

When I began working with Joseph and Craig to implement EOS, one of our initial tasks was to focus the team on accountability and getting the right people in the right seats. Through this process, Craig said, "We realized the need to be very clear with roles and responsibilities both internally and externally. We assigned titles so one person was vice president of operations and the other was vice president of business development."

The RideScout team also found value in assigning weekly to-do's and quarterly Rocks to specific individuals. "People and rocks go hand in hand," Craig said. "You take ownership of that rock and it's on you to accomplish the goal."

We'll discuss the concept of *rocks* more in a few pages. In short, it's a term for goals based on Stephen Covey's notion that it's easier to fill a glass with rocks representing your main priorities first, and then fit pebbles, sand, and water—the daily priorities—around them, than to try to fit the rocks in last.

Craig explained how using rocks helped the team overcome their tendency for everyone to pitch in and help each other out—a good trait except when it leads to overlap or gaps in performance. "I don't have time anymore to help my colleague with his rock—I'm working on my rock and he's [working on] on his," he said. "This especially resonated with our core team of four army veterans. We come from an institution that focuses on accountability, for leaders to take responsibility for their actions. It's nice to have that reinforced [in the EOS system]."

RIDESCOUT SCALES UP TO ACQUISITION

With accountability for the right people in the right seats, RideScout rapidly deployed its service in 50 U.S. cities, well on its way to delivering on Joseph's vision to rethink modern transportation around the globe. By September 2014, it was announced that Moovel GmbH, a unit of Mercedez-Benz manufacturer, Daimler AG, would purchase RideScout. The company's ability to grow quickly by leveraging the bench strength of its leaders and staff stemmed from their learning to focus on priorities for the business and each individual. "There are so many things we could be doing," Craig said. "But at the end of the day, Jonathan and EOS helped us focus."

DO YOUR PEOPLE GET IT, WANT IT, AND HAVE THE CAPACITY?

Sometimes, seats aren't filled with the right people and organizations suffer from the inertia that accompanies a stale organizational chart or one that no longer fits the size, scope, or pace of the business.

The EOS GWC tool assesses whether people:

Get it: Do they understand their role and the company?

Want it: Do they have a desire to do this job?

Capacity to Do It: Do they have the intellectual, physical, and emotional capacity to do the job well? Do they have the time?

Sometimes a leadership team struggles week after week to resolve issues around employees who are not working out; who do not have the GWC. One COO told me,

I can't tell you how many times we talked about the same people in our weekly meetings. We were spinning our wheels with people—did they get it? We'd coach them. [Finally], when we used these tools, we let people go…It's a hit, people get upset. But it's been such a relief. We've had fewer and fewer conversations about that issue.

This executive's relief is the result of using robust tools to see clearly through the issues that had dragged her organization into the dysfunctional weeds. Putting people issues into *black* and *white* terms means taking the emotion out of human resource decisions and instead focusing on what's best for the organization. What people does your company need to grow and what is the best role for each of them?

DATA: MEASURE THE RIGHT THINGS AT THE RIGHT TIME

I once worked with a commercial painting business that had 200 painters in the field. Each group on a job included a foreman and two painters. The business owners measured growth and profitability on gross margin and three inputs affected this metric: labor, materials, and equipment rentals. What happens when the foreman is not aware of how these metrics trickle down to his team's work?

In one instance, the foreman believed he needed to finish a job by Friday, so on Wednesday, he ordered three material hoists to move up and down the walls. Because success was not measured on job duration times, the equipment rental adversely impacted the gross margin. Had the foreman been aware of how his production affected margin, he could have called the project manager back at the office and requested a change in the schedule. Armed with insight into the metrics, he could raise performance by teaching his painters not to overload the brush with paint in order to reduce the materials cost for a job.

While many organizations understand the value of measuring the right stuff, they do not actually have a scorecard, dashboard, or any type of consistent system for charting their course against key indicators. In the EOS system, the Scorecard tool establishes five to fifteen high-level weekly numbers that you measure to track progress.

RideScout's Craig Cummings credits the scorecard as a "key instrument for the team." He added that selecting what is measured—what makes it onto this dashboard—is essential. His team asks whether each metric is really meaningful to help with the company's goals. "There's so much to keep track of—the scorecard helps us keep track of the right amount and the right measurables. The scorecards are the key piece for accomplishing our goals."

What gets measured gets done.

ASSIGN OWNERS FOR EACH MEASURABLE

But metrics do not exist in a vacuum. Each target needs ownership and accountability. Your company's scorecard should list the critical measurables that your team needs to take the pulse of each week such as revenue, sales activity, or customer satisfaction. Use columns to list the measurables versus the people responsible and their deadlines.

For one of my clients, their leadership holds a Monday morning meeting to review the scorecard. "We have certain things we have to report every week such as how much are we billing? Are we meeting our target? How many employees do we have? How many clients were touched this week?" said the COO. "We're all more knowledgeable." This COO also noted that the process of holding individuals accountable for metrics on the scorecard meant that everyone came into the meeting on Monday fully prepared, even if it meant they were all spending 10 to 15 minutes on Sunday night to fill in the scorecard on Google Docs with their progress against the goal.

What happens when people don't make their goals? It's common for new issues to arise and old ones to fester and prevent traction and productivity. Often, individuals and leadership teams circle around these issues in futile attempts at resolution. Learning to resolve and move beyond issues is a key component of a healthy organization and a necessary element for growth.

RESOLVE ISSUES AND MOVE ON

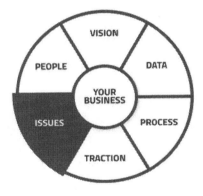

The problem with most issues is that they start out murky and only get murkier the more we discuss them. The EOS system uses a specific process for tackling issues quickly and efficiently in order to move on. It focuses on:

IDS
Identify
Discuss
Solve

This three-step process of Identify, Discuss, Solve (IDS) focuses attention on issues that are getting in the way of growth. The clearer you are in identifying particular issues, the less discussion you actually need to *solve*. A solve is not necessarily a solution; it is the next step to get to where you want to go.

One of my clients had grown more than 50% in the previous year and had several issues from high growth. One issue in particular was when its Chinese manufacturing partner kept sending more product than the client had ordered. The variance on the contract was only plus or minus 10%. But the manufacturer regularly sent plus 50%. Then they demanded payment. Why should my client burn through precious working capital to pay for product it didn't order? Here's how we used the IDS method to tackle the problem:

Identify: My client was getting too much product and couldn't store it without excess cost. Plus, the vendor was demanding payment for the non-contracted variance.

Discuss: We discussed whether it was a conflict in core values. No, it was more of a practical problem. In the back and forth discussions about the shipment quantities, the two companies had differences in language, culture, and business practices.

Solve: Our first approach was to figure out the vendor's motivation to see if their interests aligned with the client to work together. The client put themselves in their partner's shoes to see why they might be sending too much product. Yes, it was easier to run the plant. Additionally, there were cultural differences in how the contract was perceived and the plant owner felt pressure from investors to maximize profits. To align both companies' incentives, we realized that the solution was to insist on third party inspections to give the plant owner a disincentive to overrun production—any excess would be put back to the manufacturer and never make it onto the ship.

Debra Schatzki, CEO and Founder of BPP Wealth Solutions, found IDS a valuable problem-solving tool with her leadership team. "IDS is a brilliant way to help us resolve issues," she said. "You create your issues list, you prioritize them, and then you IDS each one—because there will always be issues."

Furthermore, when various issues arise, Debra and her team utilize a specific EOS tool in their solve step. "When there's a problem, like cash flow, we look in the toolbox and look for a tool to help. For example, we'd use the EOS tool, 8 cash flow drivers, to solve the issue."

YOUR PROCESS IS YOUR BUSINESS

You spend the majority of your time working "in" your business, delivering your product or service. Working "on" your business involves doing the things that help make it a resilient, stable, and valuable enterprise. Taking time to work "on" your business is a key piece of helping you gain more control and increasing its valuation.

DEFINE YOUR CORE PROCESSES

The more time that you spend working "on" your business, the easier it becomes to distinguish, simplify, document, and implement your core processes. At some point in the EOS

Process, you will look down upon your business and see that your core processes are your business—it's a franchise model—the framework that makes the economics all work.

FRONT STAGE VERSUS BACK STAGE PROCESSES

I was originally introduced to the concept of front stage and back stage processes when I attended Strategic Coach in Toronto. The entire Strategic Coach organization was intentionally designed around the concept of producing an excellent "Front Stage" show, achieved through well-documented and executed "Back Stage" processes.

Front Stage (or proven) processes represent the client-facing activities of your business: marketing, sales, and service or product delivery. This is the part of your operation that the client experiences.

BPP Wealth's proven process is the Security Income Planner™. Debra Schatzki began developing it with her coach and evolved its use when they implemented EOS. "What's been so amazing," she said, "is that the build out of our process also includes the build out of our company: What our core focus is, what that means, what it does, who we serve?"

The byproduct of determining your proven process is a one-page visual illustration of the way your organization takes care of its customers or clients. Part of your marketing strategy, your proven process is a sales and marketing tool that tells your prospects that you have a proven way of taking care of them and helps your sales team create consistent, realistic expectations.

Back Stage (or core) processes make up all of the administrative and support processes that are followed and undertaken to deliver the front stage process. This is the part of your business that happens behind closed doors.

Every business has just a handful of Core Processes – essential things that need to be done consistently well every time, no matter who in the organization is doing them. For example, most companies have an HR or people process, a marketing process, a sales process, one or more operations processes, an accounting process, and a customer service or customer retention process. Once your team agrees on your handful of core processes (and what they are going to be called forever), you must document them at a high level, train your employees, and begin measuring compliance until they are "followed by all."

Process-centric organizations have a vision and drive traction in their organization through their respect and commitment to documenting and following their processes. A process-centric organization improves performance, is change ready, and is equipped to face the pressures of the competitive market. Hero-centric organizations, on the other hand, run on the leader's drive and ambition. They lack an operating system to keep the business on course and accelerate growth. Many of my clients are initially hero-centric organizations when I meet them. Implementation of EOS is the catalyst and gateway to their transition to a process-driven enterprise.

TRACTION EQUALS ACTION

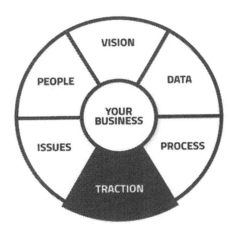

When Ford CEO Alan Mulally stepped down in July 2014, COO Mark Fields succeeded him. Fields had helped institute the One Ford vision across the company and played an important role in helping the company gain traction with the vision. Traction for Ford meant a weekly business plan review meeting, which Mulally established to track the progress of the One Ford plan and to monitor the global business and competitive environment. Field led the Thursday meetings which are credited with driving a reliable and transparent process for running Ford's global operations and enabling Ford's senior leadership to work closely together and act decisively on its plan.[2]

At EOS we focus on developing SMART Goals (Specific, Measurable, Attainable, Realistic, and Timely) to measure the quality of a company's quarterly priorities or "rocks." Rocks are the three to seven priorities you will focus on for the next ninety days. Instead of being overwhelmed with how to accomplish the big stuff by only looking at annual goals, breaking everything down into a "90-Day World" helps goals and priorities become much more manageable.

Breaking down goals into bite-sized chunks, or rocks, leaves teams free to focus on what is most important. This increased intensity and focus on clear goals is what helps leadership teams gain meaningful and measurable traction.

Company Rocks—The three to seven most important things the *company* needs to get done this quarter.

Departmental Rocks—The three to five most important things your *department* needs to accomplish this quarter.

Individual Rocks—The one to three most important things *you* need to get done this quarter.

---

2 Ford Motor Company press release, May 1, 2014.
https://media.ford.com/content/fordmedia/fna/us/en/news/2014/05/01/ford-leadership-announcement.html

When companies such as RideScout are moving fast and furiously to build a market, they risk choking on too many priorities. Co-Founder Craig Cummings said that developing rocks worked especially well for their team. The concept of rocks focuses the company, leadership team, and all employees on their vision through specific, documented goals or rocks for each week and quarter. Craig said,

> *It was just easily understood that we would say this is our rock for fourth quarter and always check to see if we accomplished those rocks. It sets a tight clean goal for individuals, provides accountability and lets everyone know what everyone's working on.*

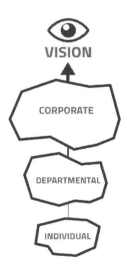

THE TRACTION TREE

Corporate rocks, the most important to ensure that the company achieves its vision, are represented at the top of the Traction Tree. The Departmental rocks are in the middle. The Individual rocks are placed at the bottom on the smallest branches of the tree. The trunk points upward since the departmental and individual rocks are in service of the corporate vision.

SET YOUR MEETING PULSE

The Meeting Pulse prescribes that leadership teams must meet weekly for 90 minutes, quarterly for a full day, and annually for two days. This enables them to stay focused, stay on the same page, and solve problems. This is how they avoid the burnout and exhaustion so common when firefighting is their daily office job.

Initially, clients balk at the notion of more meetings. By implementing the Level 10 meeting agenda, the leadership team—and eventually each department—conducts meetings that not only are not a waste of time but ensure more gets done. After all, most people procrastinate by nature. If the leadership holds quarterly meetings, they will accomplish their goals by the meeting. Now, what happens when the meetings are weekly? More gets done!

Turning quarterly rocks into weekly to-dos and holding each person accountable in the weekly meeting ensures that a majority of items gets done each week. Plus, the weekly meeting becomes an effective tool for solving issues using IDS.

LEVEL 10 MEETING AGENDA

The Level 10 meeting agenda prescribes a specific agenda for each meeting, held at the same time, on the same day, each week. This is where vision becomes action and traction for the organization. Each person is held accountable for progress toward rocks and accomplishment of his or her to-dos. Any issues and lack of success are documented and solved during the IDS portion of the meeting. You'll notice that IDS takes the bulk of the meeting time. That's because solving issues becomes the chief benefit of weekly Level 10 meetings. Remember, issues often trap an organization in stagnation. Solving these issues moves the business forward, gives it traction, and optimizes it for growth.

LEVEL 10 AGENDA

Segue: 5 min
Scorecard: 5 min
Rock Review: 5 min
Customer/Employee Headlines: 5 min
To-Do List: 5 min
IDS: 60 min
Conclude: 5 min

When Debra Schatzki's broker told her that BPP Wealth had one month to become a registered investment advisory company, she credits EOS rocks and weekly meetings with how they reached the goal. "We had to get it all up and running and transfer clients, set up an operation and billing system and our ability to service clients—better than before," she said.

> *What was an impossible task became very specific measurable goals with specific and measurable accountability. The result is that we got it up and running and billed 25% more because of the transfer. Because we had to get paperwork, clients gave us more business. After it was up and running for a year, we doubled the income.*

Or, consider RideScout's rapid transformation from startup to a scaled up business acquired by a major global transportation player. Joseph and Craig focused early on building accountability and establishing their rocks. Their ability to spread across cities stemmed from their discipline and execution. Now that's traction.

Implementing an operating system is one piece to helping your business optimize for growth. It's equally important to build traction and accountability for your leadership with additional outside perspective. A strong peer network balances your internal growth with external input. In the next chapter, we'll explore how you can build this into your plan to grow.

HOW DO YOU RATE ON OPTIMIZING YOUR BUSINESS?

Take the following assessment on the next page to determine your current strengths and weaknesses regarding your business strategy, operations, and infrastructure. You may also take the assessment online at www.chiefoptimizer.com/assessment.

OPERATING SYSTEM ASSESSMENT

For each statement below, rank your business on a scale of 1 to 5, where 1 is weak and 5 is strong.

	1	2	3	4	5
1. Your business is aligned around a plan.	○	○	○	○	○
2. We have the right people in the right seats.	○	○	○	○	○
3. Our leadership team has a regularly scheduled offsite meeting to work "on" the business.	○	○	○	○	○
4. We have well defined metrics to track business results.	○	○	○	○	○
5. Our processes are documented and followed by all.	○	○	○	○	○
6. There is a solid culture of accountability in our organization.	○	○	○	○	○
7. Our meetings have clear objectives, agendas and follow up items.	○	○	○	○	○

8. We clearly prioritize identify, discuss and solve all key issues for the greater, long-term good. ○ ○ ○ ○ ○

9. We effectively cascade messages from the leadership team to their direct reports and throughout the entire company. ○ ○ ○ ○ ○

10. We have quarterly conversations with all employees to reinforce core values, review quarterly goals and clarify their roles. ○ ○ ○ ○ ○

Total number of each rating

x2	x4	x6	x8	x10

Multiply by number above

Add all five numbers to determine the percentage score that reflects the current state of your company ⬚ %. An Operating System Assessment score of 80 or higher is considered strong.

CHAPTER 3

OPTIMIZE YOUR NETWORK

*If I have seen further it is by standing
on the shoulders of giants.*
ISAAC NEWTON

When the Walt Disney Company added Facebook COO Sheryl Sandberg to its board in 2009, she joined executives, some who had retired, from Seagram, Estee Lauder, Twitter, and U.S. Hispanic Media, among others. Together, they bring valuable perspective from relevant brands and industries to advise Disney on its strategy and opportunities for success. Sure, Disney's a media powerhouse with the clout to assemble top names for its board. But why shouldn't entrepreneurs benefit from the wisdom of a wisely assembled group of peers who can share their experiences from the perspective of a similar company size and leadership role?

More so, how handicapped is the small business leader who does not have a peer advisory network?

Disney and other public companies have Boards of Directors (BoD) to hold them accountable to their corporate vision and targets, and to provide valuable, outside perspective on the critical challenges their businesses face each quarter. Just because your business is smaller than Disney, and private, does not mean having a trusted group of peer advisors is not an essential component of success. It's the second leg of the Optimize for Growth Model for an important reason: An entrepreneur alone is an entrepreneur at risk.

Peer advisory networks consist of other business leaders, like yourself, who can help problem solve issues and test ideas from their vantage points of similar roles, industries, or business size. Some leaders may have more experience than you; some may have less. The power of the group input, from varying perspectives, gives you traction to resolve issues, gain new ideas, and leverage the wisdom of their collective experience.

OPTIMIZE YOUR NETWORK WITH PEER ADVISORY

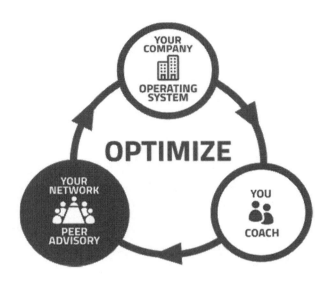

THE POWER OF GROUP THINK

At my former company, Wave Dispersion Technologies, Inc., we had a situation in which a client refused to pay a $50,000 invoice. The client's company had gone bankrupt and we wanted both payment from them as well as controls to prevent similar situations in the future.

At the time, I was a member of a peer advisory group through the Entrepreneur's Organization (EO), a global peer-to-peer network of entrepreneurs. In my local Detroit chapter, I was a member of a "Forum," a member-led, confidential, peer-sharing program that consisted of owners of similar-size businesses from a range of non-competitive industries and backgrounds. EO's philosophy centers around confidential peer-to-peer sharing based on individual experience, known as "gestalt protocol" and not on "advice." The magic lies in the realization that there is often another member who has expertise or experience around the issue or decision you are grappling with in your company.

I told my EO Forum group about the problem. One of the members suggested that we always put a UCC 1 Statement filing—a mortgage instrument that secures the lender's/vendor's claim—to the assigned collateral (e.g., the materials sold to the customer). I wished I had known this before I sold to the client that went bankrupt. I immediately put a process in place to secure a UCC filing on all future sales of $50,000 or greater where we had any concern about counterparty credit worthiness. In essence, the input from my "peers" catapulted me up the entrepreneur's typical learning curve. I took the elevator instead of the stairs.

IMPROVE YOUR ODDS OF SUCCESS

Six months after founding his sales consulting firm, Imagine Business Development, Doug Davidoff faced a high degree of uncertainty. During this time, Vistage, a peer advisory company where groups of up to sixteen members meet for a full day with a guest speaker, invited him to speak at one of its local group meetings. After doing so, Doug realized that this type of peer networking group would be valuable for the stage he was at with his business.

"I benefitted a lot from Vistage," he said. "In the beginning, I learned that successful business owners had as much uncertainty as I had. There was no magic answer."

While he admits to having some nervousness with the group early on, he eventually learned to share within the group, and that his concern that he didn't have the experience to make certain types of business decisions was the norm. "It didn't feel so strange," he said.

Doug sums up his peer network benefits as:

1. Advancing His Learning Curve
   One of the advantages is that you get to see and experience so many people's issues that when you're dealing with things on a day-to-day basis, they're less serious.

2. Confronting Potential Issues Ahead of Time
   When issues arose, especially when it came to dealing with people, I felt more comfortable. I had had the meeting in my head ahead of time. Within a year period, 90% of what happens to me has happened to someone in the group.

3. Test Decisions
   After two years, my company decided to make a bold strategic move. I put the idea in front of my Vistage group to get feedback. Of the 17 people in the room, 14 said it was a risky idea. But I had dealt with every issue they brought up. I realized that I had thought it through as much as I could and it was time to put it into practice. We had our first client within two weeks.

Doug said,

> *At the end of the day I want to know if I'm asking the right question. A peer group lets you find that space where you've thought it through enough. It allows you to make faster decisions with more confidence.*

TYPES OF PEER GROUPS

Chances are one of the several peer network organizations has a local membership group near you. Peer advisory groups come in a wide range of shapes, colors, and sizes. Some are very formal with substantial membership dues, formal bylaws, and strict membership criteria. Others are free, with loose guiding principles and easy entry. You can likely find a peer group, no matter where you live: inquire at the Chamber of Commerce, your local house of worship, or on the Internet. Below is a sample list of some well known peer advisory groups:

ENTREPRENEURS' ORGANIZATION (EO)

EO, which I joined after founding my first startup, focuses on entrepreneurs and members lead its groups. EO also provides opportunities for executive education, mentorships, and global events. The organization's philosophy of gestalt guides members to provide input from their own business experience rather than advice for its own sake.

HELM

Helm brings CEOs together in ultra-personalized groups to stop wasting time, money and stress finding solutions. Helm CEOs help each other not just in finding answers but also in finding the questions. Experienced CEOs know: you don't know what you don't know, but others do. And with the right group, virtually any problem can be solved.

RENAISSANCE EXECUTIVE FORUMS

Renaissance Executive Forums in an international peer group organization for company CEOs, Presidents and Owners. Renaissance brings together top executives from non-competing companies of similar size, into an peer advisory forum. Member participate in monthly meetings, quarterly coaching and an annual learning and planning retreats from which thousands of leaders report gaining fresh ideas and new insights. Each Forum is facilitated by a trained and experienced Forum Leader. In addition to programs for CEOs, Renaissance offers peer forums for key executives who are often the direct reports of the CEO and assessment tools for the business and its managers.

THE ALTERNATIVE BOARD (TAB)

TAB targets local small/medium-sized business owners who run non-competing businesses with group sizes of five to ten members. Each board is formed and facilitated by a Certified Business Coach/Facilitator and meets once a month. Members may also opt to meet with the facilitator for private coaching.

VISTAGE

Vistage is known for its CEO and small business forums of up to sixteen members in similar-sized companies across industries. An experienced Vistage Chair facilitates each monthly, full day meeting. Members also receive monthly private executive coaching from the Chair. The global organization provides groups for development of key

WOMEN'S PRESIDENTS ORGANIZATION (WPO)

WPO is a non-profit organization for women presidents of multimillion-dollar companies. The professionally facilitated peer group meetings help female leaders achieve success both as women and for their organizations.

YOUNG PRESIDENTS ORGANIZATION (YPO)

YPO, the global networking organization of company leaders under 45 years of age, hosts forums, events, mentoring programs, and learning events across 125 countries. YPO's prestige gives members access to corporate and government leaders and active social communities for networking and growth. YPO focuses on the "whole person" and emphasizes both the personal and professional fulfillment from membership.
executives within companies as well.

PEER NETWORK CRITERIA

Selecting a peer group often comes down to finding the right fit for you. However, it's important that your group consists of members with similar:

Company size —A $2M cannot relate to $50M business owners, but will learn from $15 million owners.
Authority—Are other members also running their own business with final say for strategic direction, hard decisions, and employee issues?

Goals—Do they want purely professional development, family and business, or personal growth? This may not be apparent at the outset, but eventually the group dynamics will reflect its members' goals.

And of course this is a strictly confidential environment consisting of similarly sized non-competitive companies.

FORCED ACCOUNTABILITY

Whichever type of group you choose, the chief benefit of a peer network is the forced accountability it gives you toward your strategy, goals, and execution. Some leaders remain in peer groups for years, and longevity has its benefits for the trust and sharing that comes with relationships developed over a period of time. Other leaders find that they outgrow their groups and migrate to new groups to match the changes in their business, stage of life, and personal goals.

Eventually, you may develop the networking skills and relationships to form ad hoc peer groups on your own, entrusting a select group of trusted advisors to be your sounding board for key decisions and issues as they arise. It's essential to continue to leverage peers for ongoing feedback to balance your views on the business.

In addition to leveraging a peer network, entrepreneurs must also develop their personal leadership skills. Leading at the top can be a lonely endeavor. Often, there's no one available to understand and coach you on the specific issues a leader encounters day to day and during crises. To give you the maximum traction for your personal leadership, it's important to work with an executive coach, who holds you accountable to your near- and long-term professional and personal goals. This is the subject of our next chapter.

HOW DO YOU RATE ON OPTIMIZING YOUR NETWORK?

Take the following assessment on the next page to determine the strengths and weaknesses of your peer network. You may also take the assessment online at www.chiefoptimizer.com/ assessment.

OPERATING SYSTEM ASSESSMENT

For each statement below, rank your peer network on a scale of 1 to 5, where 1 is weak and 5 is strong.

		1	2	3	4	5
1.	I have a close network of business owners that I can confide in when I have a major issue.	○	○	○	○	○
2.	I have a group that asks me the tough questions that are in my blind spot.	○	○	○	○	○
3.	I regularly meet with a mastermind group to help me achieve success.	○	○	○	○	○
4.	I am open to both giving and receiving support in a group environment.	○	○	○	○	○
5.	I have a trusted group of peers outside my industry with which I brainstorm and share experience.	○	○	○	○	○
6.	I am willing to be vulnerable and share my weaknesses in a confidential peer setting.	○	○	○	○	○

7. I have a documented plan for my leadership development. ○ ○ ○ ○ ○

8. I see the value of sharing for both my peers and myself. ○ ○ ○ ○ ○

9. I belong to a group that is committed to shared goals of professional and company improvement and setting a course for the future ○ ○ ○ ○ ○

10. I regularly share best practices and ideas with a group of peers. ○ ○ ○ ○ ○

Total number of each rating

x2	x4	x6	x8	x10

Multiply by number above

Add all five numbers to determine the percentage score that reflects the current state of your peer network ⬚ %. A Peer Advisory Assessment score of 80 or higher is considered strong.

CHAPTER 4

OPTIMIZE YOU

Everybody needs a coach.
ERIC SCHMIDT
EXECUTIVE CHAIRMAN OF GOOGLE

I still remember the day I got my "ticket" to fly, in the form of my pilot's license. My flight instructor, with a proud yet knowing smile said, "Your pilot's license is a ticket to continue to learn, not a validation of your piloting skills." I've spent the last 20+ years and over 1,000 flight hours becoming a pilot and I've continued my flight education throughout that time, working with countless flight instructors in order to obtain licenses, ratings, and endorsements. To ensure that I'm the best pilot I can be, I'm continually working on sharpening my skills.

Although I've worked with a variety of instructors over the years, I've always maintained a very close relationship with my original instructor who is affectionately known by my family as our own "Pilot Bill." Bill isn't just a talented pilot in practice, he and I have developed a rhythm of communication pre- and post-flight to review my flight plan, my personal minimums checklist, and often to debrief me on my decision-making process after a particularly challenging or stressful flight.

Learning to fly, much like operating a business, is a truly dynamic experience. I don't know if I would have survived my flying adventures without my trusted flying advisor relationship with Bill. As it also turns out, I don't know many successful organizations that haven't benefitted from the guidance of a portfolio of trusted advisors.

Entrepreneurs, by nature, already have the basic flying skills, but they need the support and wisdom of their trusted advisors to learn the more advanced skills that make them high-impact leaders. Taking risks right out of the gate, either in a plane or in a business, without a trusted advisor providing guidance along the way is an incredibly risky way to operate.

As we've discussed, trusted outsiders can take the form of a coach, a peer networking group, or an implementer for an operating system. Many entrepreneurs start with a coach and some use them in conjunction with a peer network group or to help implement their operating system. The best approach for you depends on your unique set of hurdles and current business priorities.

OPTIMIZE YOURSELF WITH A COACH

TOP LEADERS LEVERAGE COACHES

Google CEO Eric Schmidt said in this popular Fortune video, "One thing people are never good at is seeing themselves as others see them. A coach really, really helps."

The well-known executive coach, <u>Marshall Goldsmith</u>, worked with Ford CEO Alan Mulally when he was still at Boeing. Most top executives work with coaches, and large institutions typically have a senior organizational development role; a person who works with the executive team to develop leadership skills and resolve issues.

Think of your coach as your leadership support system. A coach helps you shape your approach to the organization and the people in it and provides the wisdom and guidance to effectively resolve issues and overcome challenges. Your coach gives you the buffer to stay focused on leading the organization.

I recently met with Lieutenant General (Ret.) David Huntoon Jr, who led the training of our military officers at West Point and is now President of D2H Consulting. As David described it to me, "Coaching and mentoring are continuous requirements in any organization that values growth, adapting to the extraordinary change we see in the marketplace today."

David noted that the military values and reinforces leadership development through a continuous cycle of training, development, coaching, and mentorship of leaders from their first day in service and as they move upward. "Coaching and mentoring is a very effective reinforcing technique in leader development." He said. "The opportunity to take a complex leadership concern to a trusted superior allows you to lay out your issue in complete candor and gain the wisdom of greater experience without being judged."

THE READINESS FACTOR

Working with a coach requires some readiness on your part. Are you open to asking frank questions of yourself? Will you experiment with new approaches to working with your colleagues and staff? Are you willing to be held accountable to your goals?

A good coaching relationship:

1. Opens your mind to possibility and fosters the mindset to succeed
2. Provides an objective sounding board—"Shines the Light"
3. Holds you accountable to your goals
4. Brings experience—the coach has been in your shoes before
5. Helps you create a legacy—think bigger than you do

When Erica Marrari was promoted to VP, Client Services at 5AM Solutions, she sought out a coach who had paved her way in a similar career path. "I wanted some assistance with managing the role, being an executive at the company, and how I was going to grow as a woman in customer service in technology and science," she said. "I realized it had more to do with style more than anything else."

Erica asked me to help her find a female coach who had a background in science or technology product development. I recommended Cindy Morgan, former vice president of organizational development and learning at NYU Langone Medical Center and now Vice President, Learning & Organization Development, Penn Medicine (University of Pennsylvania Health System). Cindy didn't have the specific industry background Erica was seeking, but she fit several other criteria and was in a related field.

Erica gathered more names from her network and eventually interviewed over seven coach candidates. She chose Cindy because of her approach. "Cindy suggested that we focus on the here and now and then make my 5 to 10 year plan," Erica said.

According to Cindy, the top reasons individuals engage coaches are:

1. Taking on a new role, for example, going from peer to boss
2. Entering a strong culture from the outside
3. As a senior leader (e.g., the executive team)

"When you have people that rise up in the organization," she said, "it's hard to find the right course to teach them the specifics of what to know. It needs to be specific to the person's context. If you can accelerate by increasing your self-awareness during a time of transition, you can exponentially grow and enter jobs, and business relationships more intentionally."

A GUIDE WHO SHINES THE LIGHT

To change your behavior, it's important to understand the context and culture in which you're operating and a coach can help you ascertain how you come at it. "If you look at a situation differently once your awareness is raised," she said, "You can come at it from a different angle."

For Erica, that meant learning how to avoid and manage conflicts. "A lot of it centers around language," she noted. "I'm a direct person and Cindy would coach me on how to use alternative language for more of a soft landing. It was about changing the way that I phrased things, asking more questions, and being more analytical."

Cindy role-played with Erica so that she could learn new approaches with her colleagues through practice. "I've had a lot of people give me guidance but never in that way," Erica said. "It was very useful."

GROW WITH YOUR CIRCUMSTANCES

Alicia Marie, founder of People Biz, a coaching and training organization, said that the number one reason people decide to engage a coach is that they hit a personal development ceiling. A moment occurs when they are stuck, when they realize they must change in order to be successful. "That can happen because your entire team of twelve just walked out on you, or you just sold $1 million in product and can't fund it," Marie said.

"It can be due to major success or major issues." Either way, the person acknowledges that they will have to grow to deal with the circumstance.

Alicia Marie noted that the biggest challenge is always people:

You can have systems in place but what people underestimate is that people are the levers. I've seen people with all sorts of resources fail because they weren't paying attention to the people. Anyone can be successful by him or herself. But can you get another person to his or her optimum level? That takes skill. Until leaders and managers can do that, they're at a disadvantage. Companies that do that will have a huge advantage. That's where coaching comes in.

Plus, for entrepreneurs and senior leaders at emerging growth companies, there are fewer people to talk to and be authentic with about your struggles on the path to scaling up. "Good coaches ask great questions at the right time," said Cindy Morgan. "And slow you down before you take action that may or may not help you in the long run."

GAIN PERSONAL TRACTION

Fourteen years ago, Mark Huge, executive coach and founder of Work Flow Facilitators, volunteered at a Cleveland clinic with a doctor to help patients resolve their personal and business issues. After a couple of years, Mark said to the doctor, "We talk about the issues each week and the next week the patients have the same problem. We need to put some structure in to help them solve those problems and hold them accountable to that."

Afterward, Mark and the doctor developed what they call the *OCE system* (Order, Control, Execute) to help people get organized and in control of their tasks, goals, and issues. "No one person can do it all," Mark says. "When people get overwhelmed, they need a system. There's always more to be done than can be done."

I have worked with Mark for several years and one of the key values I find in having a coach is that he both knows my vision and what I'm up to week to week. This proves invaluable when the inevitable crises emerge. In other words, not only is he available to me for one-on-one coaching to work through an issue, he also has the context to guide me through a fork in the road.

This came in handy recently when a partner from my former business asked me to pursue an opportunity. Tempting as it was to take on, I didn't want to lose the momentum I've driven developing the Optimize for Growth system and helping my clients implement it in their own organizations.

Mark reminded me, "A year ago this is what we agreed it [my vision and business] looks like. Stay on task."

That simple reflection helped me stay focused and make the right choice when I didn't have the horsepower or objectivity to effectively tackle the challenge myself.

Dave Marinac, owner of ABC Packaging Direct, also works with Mark Huge to implement EOS in his organization. "Mark leads our Level 10 meetings every Monday," Dave said. "He helps us to keep the emotion out of it. I want to jump in, as an entrepreneur, but he keeps us on point." In addition, Dave uses him for general executive coaching. "He's the guy I call with work issues and to bounce ideas off of him," he shared.

Mark Huge emphasizes that being successful does not negate the need for a coach. "Mike Phelps has a coach with him virtually all the time —he's with him in the pool," he commented. "Why does he need a coach being as good as he is? He needs a coach to help him stay on track. He makes his money swimming. If he has to think of all the other pieces and parts, he won't be as effective swimming. Everyone needs a coach to be truly productive and fulfilled."

CHOOSING A COACH

Coaches vary and choosing one takes forethought and due diligence. To begin, ask your mentor(s) and extended network for recommendations based on a set of criteria you have already developed (e.g., gender, background, focus, etc.). Interview each candidate by phone to gauge your comfort level and the chemistry and type of dialog that ensues.

Cindy Morgan suggests that you ask yourself some basic questions: Can I be my worst self with this person? "This isn't about pleasing and putting your best face on. It's about being real," she said. Additionally, she asks potential clients, "Why coaching and why now?"

Often, the impetus for finding a coach occurs when entrepreneurs hit their personal ceiling. This may be coupled with a struggle in the business or a realization that what got you here will not get you there. There's another way: select a coach as part of your decision to implement the Optimize for Growth system. Your desire to scale up drove you to read this book. Now it is time to assess your top priorities for achieving growth and begin your journey on an efficient and effective path to scaling up.

HOW DO YOU RATE ON OPTIMIZING YOURSELF?

Take the following assessment to determine the strengths and weaknesses of your professional development and support. You may also take the assessment online at www.chiefoptimizer. com/assessment.

COACHING ASSESSMENT

For each statement below, rank your coaching on a scale of 1 to 5, where 1 is weak and 5 is strong.

		1	2	3	4	5
1.	I have more than enough time in the day to accomplish my to-do list.	○	○	○	○	○
2.	I have all of the knowledge, skills, confidence and resources I need to lead at work, home and in the community.	○	○	○	○	○
3.	I have an independent seasoned professional, not an employee, who is in my corner helping me prioritize opportunities and challenges as they arise.	○	○	○	○	○
4.	My work / life is in balance.	○	○	○	○	○
5.	I have someone I go to when I am feeling stuck.	○	○	○	○	○
6.	I am clear about my core strengths and am good at delegation.	○	○	○	○	○

7. I have someone who is helping me accelerate my personal and professional results.

   ○ ○ ○ ○ ○

8. I have someone to go to with difficult decisions and helps me weigh the pros and cons.

   ○ ○ ○ ○ ○

9. I am open minded and willing to take advice from someone who has walked in my shoes.

   ○ ○ ○ ○ ○

10. I have lofty goals and could benefit from someone holding me accountable to achieving them.

    ○ ○ ○ ○ ○

Total number of each rating

x2 x4 x6 x8 x10

Multiply by number above

Add all five numbers to determine the percentage score that reflects your coaching state ☐ %. A Coaching Assessment score of 80 or higher is considered strong.

CHAPTER 5

OPTIMIZE TODAY

Innovation is rewarded. Execution is worshipped.
DAN GILBERT
FOUNDER AND CHAIRMAN OF QUICKEN LOANS, INC.

The willingness and ability to shift from hitting the ceiling to scaling up is both a mindset to grow your organization and a discipline to putting the right methods and set of trusted advisors in place to do so. Large organizations have these structures in place. So does the military. Lieutenant General (Ret.) David Huntoon Jr, who I spoke about in chapter 4, put it this way,

> *Leadership development begins from the moment you take your first platoon in the U.S. Army as a new lieutenant. It is all about building that team, communicating the vision and mission, helping them achieve their goals and objectives through training, coaching, and mentoring,*

and setting the conditions for their ownership of your command intent. When done well, this leadership development creates successful, high performing organizations.

If you and your organization are faced with the issues we've discussed throughout the book, ask yourself what risks you are taking by not implementing the Optimize for Growth Model. What opportunities will you miss?

Each leader and his or her organization experience their own unique hurdles. Document your key takeaways from each chapter to help you assess and prioritize your current pain points and areas where you're hitting the ceiling. Consider these points to develop a plan for acquiring the trusted advisors necessary to help you take the elevator instead of the stairs.

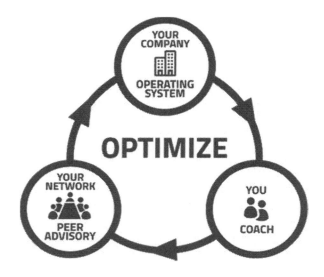

Where you are on your path and the specific issues taxing your energy and productivity will determine the takeaways that resonate most for you. You do not have to tackle all three areas of the Optimize for Growth Model at once. Start with your most pressing areas inhibiting growth and build from there. It is likely that as you build resources to develop your business, your network, or yourself, the other areas will naturally develop. You will also probably realize how much each area will benefit from its own Optimize for Growth plan. And when you invest in a coordinated plan to scale up, you will meet your business goals more quickly, with purposeful efficiency, and achieve better results. Write down your rocks. Create your to-do list. Begin optimizing for growth today.

Would you like to determine the next steps you need to make to optimize your business for growth? Review your answers to the assessments at the end of each chapter or take our online assessment today at http://www.chiefoptimizer.com/assessment. Or, contact us at:

Jonathan B. Smith
2753 Broadway, Suite 234
New York, NY 10025

+1(917) 288-2440
jonathan@chiefoptimizer.com

ABOUT THE AUTHOR

Jonathan B. Smith, entrepreneur, author and Certified EOS Implementer, is Founder and CEO of Chief Optimizer where he helps entrepreneurs scale up, beyond startup. A former Inc. 500 COO, he scaled his business from $500K to $15 million in five years and now advises entrepreneurs who have "hit the ceiling." Today, Jonathan applies his Division III varsity football experience to build high performance entrepreneurial leadership teams and help them achieve their vision. Learn more at www.chiefoptimizer.com.

Proof

Made in the USA
Charleston, SC
10 August 2016